# ELEPHANTS

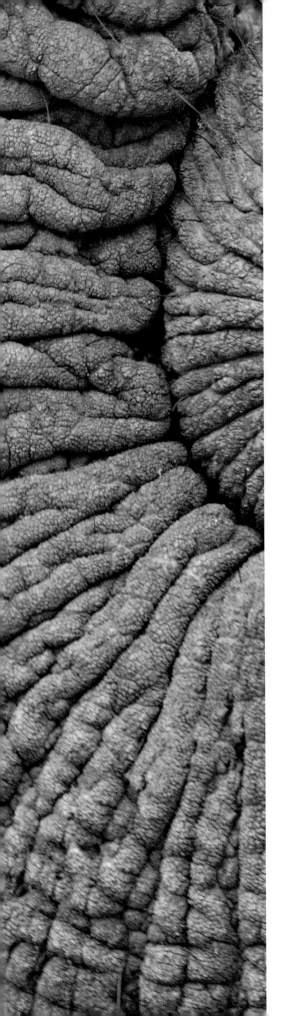

# LIVING WILD

Published by Creative Education

P.O. Box 227, Mankato, Minnesota 56002

Creative Education is an imprint of The Creative Company

www.thecreativecompany.us

Design and production by Mary Herrmann

Art direction by Rita Marshall

Printed in the United States of America

Photographs by 123RF (Steffen Foerster, Valery Shanin, Nico Smit), Alamy (The London Art Archive, Ann and Steve Toon, Maximilian Weinzierl), Corbis (Kapoor Baldev/Sygma, Jonathan Blair, David Higgs/Sygma, Craig Lovell), Dreamstime (Joseppi, Mkerkez, Mschalke, Outdoorsman), Getty Images (Chris du Plessis, Beverly Joubert, Panoramic Images, Michael Poliza, Paul Raae/FPG, Christopher Scott, Art Wolfe), iStockphoto (Steven Allan, Neil Bradfield, Rob Broek, Nikita Golovanov, Robert Hardholt, Megan Ironside, Herbert Kratky, Sunil Kumar, Peter Malsbury, Jurie Maree, Jeremy Richards, Mark Rigby), Minden Pictures (Patricio Robles Gil/Sierra Madre)

Library of Congress Cataloging-in-Publication Data

Gish, Melissa.

Elephants / by Melissa Gish.

p. cm. — (Living wild)

Includes bibliographical references and index.

ISBN 978-1-58341-739-3

1. Elephants—Juvenile literature. I. Title. II. Series.

QL737.P98G57 2009

599.67—dc22    2008009503

First Edition

9 8 7 6 5 4 3 2 1

**CREATIVE EDUCATION**

# ELEPHANTS

Melissa Gish

A trail of dust blows upward and swirls

away from the parched earth,

revealing the trail of an elephant herd.

A trail of dust blows upward and swirls away from the parched earth, revealing the trail of an elephant herd. It is midsummer in Zimbabwe, a country in southeastern Africa, and the savanna has been without rain for more than six months. The elephants' instincts draw them toward rain falling on the far horizon. Other animals such as zebras and gazelles have joined in the long trek in search of water. A young mother elephant and her calf struggle to keep up with the herd. Lions

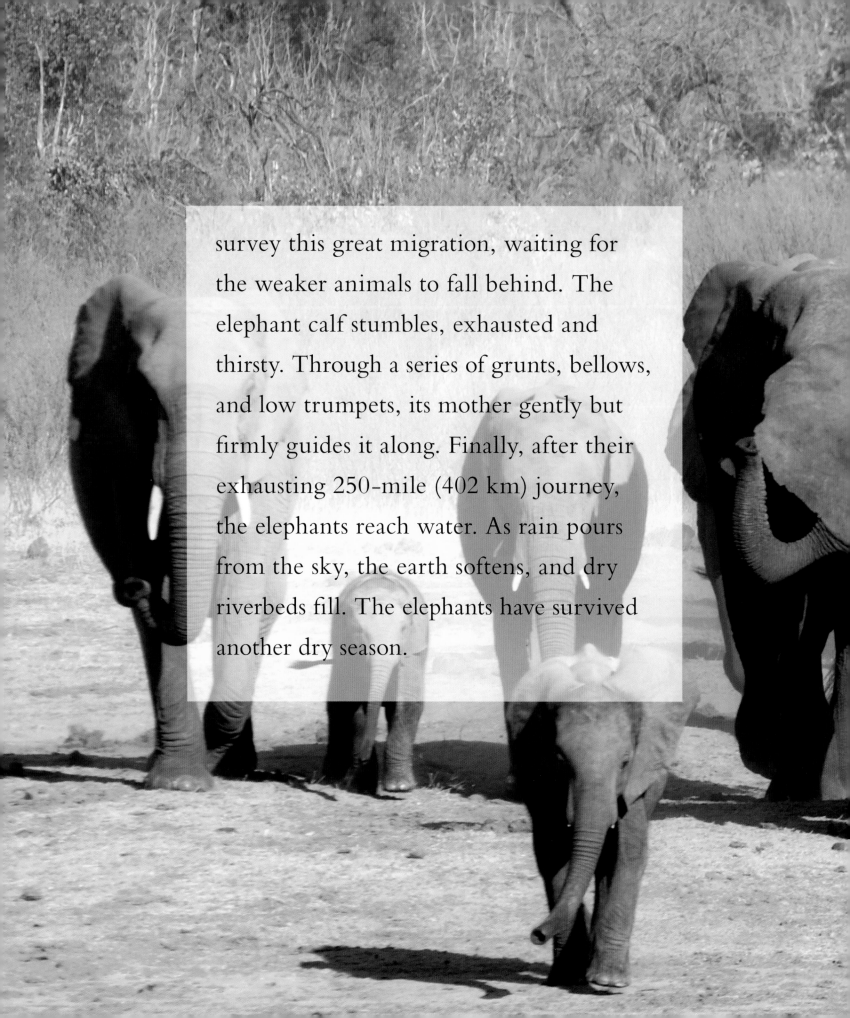

survey this great migration, waiting for the weaker animals to fall behind. The elephant calf stumbles, exhausted and thirsty. Through a series of grunts, bellows, and low trumpets, its mother gently but firmly guides it along. Finally, after their exhausting 250-mile (402 km) journey, the elephants reach water. As rain pours from the sky, the earth softens, and dry riverbeds fill. The elephants have survived another dry season.

## WHERE IN THE WORLD THEY LIVE

**Asian Elephant**
Bangladesh, southern India, Sri Lanka, Indochina, and parts of Indonesia

**African Forest Elephant**
tropical rainforests of western and central Africa

**African Bush Elephant**
savannas of central and southern Africa

Three species—African bush, African forest, and Asian—make up the population of elephants living in the world today. As represented by the colored squares, elephants can be found in their native lands of Africa, southern Asia, and southeastern Asia.

## PEACEFUL GIANTS

Elephants are the largest animals that live on land. The earliest elephant ancestors appeared about 50 million years ago and developed into more than 350 species. However, only three species of elephant exist today: African bush, African forest, and Asian elephants. Today's elephants are related to the now-extinct **mammoths** of Earth's last ice age, which ended about 10,000 years ago. The closest living relatives of elephants today are the rabbit-sized hyrax and the aquatic manatee.

Elephants and their relatives are mammals. All mammals, with the exception of the platypus and the hedgehog-like echidnas, give birth to live offspring and produce milk to feed their young. Mammals are warm-blooded animals. This means that their bodies have to work to maintain a healthy temperature. Elephants cool down by flapping their ears like fans to release heat from their bodies. They also sweat between their toes. Long eyelashes help filter out dust from the air, and thick, flexible skin protects elephants from wind, rain, and heat. Elephants can tolerate cold temperatures as long as their skin remains dry. They have hair, but it is patchy and

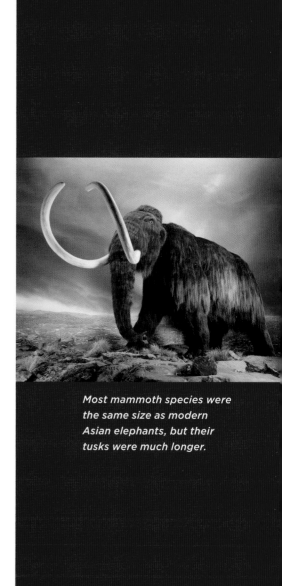

*Most mammoth species were the same size as modern Asian elephants, but their tusks were much longer.*

An adult African elephant's trunk is about eight feet (2.4 m) long and can hold up to 2.6 gallons (10 l) of water.

thin. The longest hairs are on the tip of an elephant's tail.

An elephant's trunk is its most striking feature. It is an **adaptation** of the nose and upper lip and has two nostrils through which the elephant breathes. The trunk is made up of about 40,000 muscles, making it incredibly flexible. It can be used to carry food to the mouth, or it can be used as a defensive weapon. An adult male elephant can lift up to 600 pounds (272 kg) with his trunk. The trunk is also used to investigate the environment. Raising its trunk into the air, an elephant can detect the smells of its herd, other herds, and potential predators. Female elephants even use their trunks to discipline their young, smacking them with warnings to avoid danger.

Both male and female elephants develop tusks. Tusks are actually long teeth that stick out when the elephant's mouth is closed. Inside the mouth are just four flat teeth. These teeth can be up to 4 inches (10 cm) wide and 12 inches (30.5 cm) long. As elephants grind their food, their teeth get worn down. When an elephant is about 15 years old, a second set of teeth pushes up from beneath the first set, which then falls out. These new teeth last for roughly 15 to 25 years. After that, the elephant will get two more

*A coating of mud protects elephants against not only sunburn but also parasites—animals that might live on and harm an elephant.*

*Valued for their large, ivory tusks, bull elephants lead insecure lives, constantly in danger of being hunted.*

sets, each lasting up to 20 years. When an old elephant cannot properly grind its food anymore, it will eventually starve to death. Most African elephants do not live past the age of 80, and Asian elephants rarely live past 60.

Elephants are herbivores, which means that they eat only plants, leaves, grass, seeds, and fruits. If they cannot reach the leaves, elephants may push over trees. Elephants that live near people may even steal crops. Yet most elephants serve an important role in their habitats. Many of the seeds that an elephant eats are not fully digested.

When these seeds are excreted by the elephant, they can grow into new plants and trees. An elephant can eat about 500 pounds (227 kg) of food and drink about 50 gallons (189 l) of water per day. To reach a water source, elephants may have to walk great distances. Elephants walk about 4 miles (6.4 km) per hour, but an angry or frightened elephant can run 25 miles (40 km) per hour, easily chasing predators away from its herd.

Up until the late 20th century, scientists believed that only two species of elephant existed: African and Asian. But closer studies of elephants' **DNA** in 2000 revealed that African elephants could be divided into two distinct species, bush (*Loxodonta africana*) and forest (*Loxodonta cyclotis*) elephants. These two species differ in their size, the shapes of their ears and mouths, and the number of toenails on their feet.

Male African bush elephants can grow to be 10 to 13 feet (3–4 m) high at the shoulder and can weigh up to 18,000 pounds (8 t). (Female elephants are about three-quarters of the size of males.) Their ivory tusks have been used to make tools and artifacts for thousands of years. The bush elephant is also called the savanna elephant

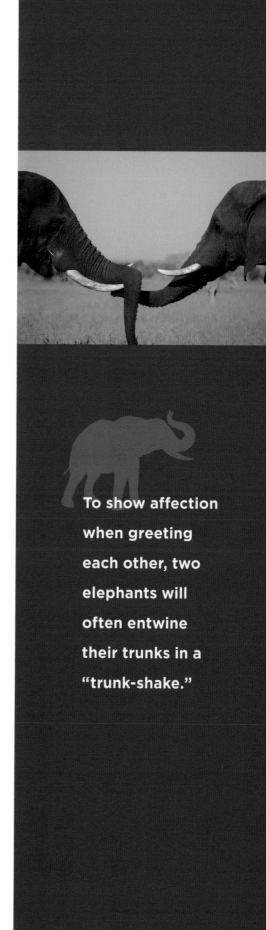

To show affection when greeting each other, two elephants will often entwine their trunks in a "trunk-shake."

because it lives on the savannas, or open plains, of the countries of Kenya, Tanzania, Botswana, Zimbabwe, Namibia, and South Africa.

African forest elephants have adapted to life in dense jungles. They are slightly smaller and stouter than bush elephants and have longer, narrower mouths. Since large curved tusks might get caught on jungle vines and tree branches, forest elephants gradually developed smaller, thinner, and straighter tusks. Also, forest elephants have five hooves on the front foot and four on the back foot, whereas bush elephants have four hooves on the front foot and three on the back foot. Forest elephants can be found from the central African country of Congo west to Mauritania. Both kinds of African elephants need a large territory in which to live and find enough food. An elephant's territory, or home range, covers about 1,240 square miles (3,212 sq km).

The third elephant species, the Asian elephant (*Elephas maximus*), is native to the wetlands and grasslands of Indonesia, Bangladesh, India, southern China, and Indochina. It is smaller than the African elephants, rarely reaching more than 10 feet (3 m) tall at the shoulder and

weighing up to 12,000 pounds (5.4 t). The Asian elephant is considered an endangered species and is at risk of **extinction**. Researchers estimate that only about 28,000 to 42,000 Asian elephants now exist in the wild.

One obvious physical characteristic that can be used to tell the three species of elephant apart is the ears. African bush elephants have triangular-shaped ears with pointy ends. African forest elephants have more rounded ears. Both species of African elephant have ears so large that they cover the neck. Asian elephants' ears are much smaller and do not cover the neck.

*Each elephant's ears are unique; researchers treat the ears as fingerprints and use them to identify individuals.*

*Elephant families take care of each other; if calves become orphaned, they are adopted by aunts or sisters.*

## FAMILY VALUES

Most elephants live in groups called herds. Female elephants, called cows, run the family herds. An older, more experienced female—the matriarch—watches over females and young males who are related to her. A herd may consist of 6 to 12 family members and may grow to include 20 to 40 elephants from other families. If herds get too big and food becomes scarce, family members may break from their existing herd to form a new herd that will move into a different territory. When a matriarch dies, one of her daughters takes over.

Male elephants are called bulls. When bulls become teenagers, they leave the family herd. Up to 15 bulls may join together to form a "bull band." Elephant society is based on **hierarchy**. Each animal fits into a particular role, with some having more power than others. Bulls fight each other for dominance. By fighting over access to food and water—and building up their strength—older, bigger bulls gain power over younger bulls.

When a male elephant matures between the ages of 10 and 15, he is old enough to mate. Around this time,

**The elephant symbol of the Republican Party in America was created by cartoonist Thomas Nast and first appeared in 1874.**

**Elephants are strong swimmers and can use their trunks as snorkels to breathe underwater when crossing deep lakes or rivers.**

the bull starts producing high levels of a chemical called testosterone, which causes the elephant to become more aggressive and want to mate soon. During periods when they produce the most testosterone, male elephants leave the bull band to seek out herds with females who are also ready to mate. Elephants do not have a specific mating season, so this can occur at any time.

When they reach 10 to 15 years of age, cows will begin to mate with dominant males that visit their herd, and they may continue to breed into their 50s. After mating, the bull leaves the herd and returns to his bull band. He will have nothing to do with the raising of his offspring. The cow carries her single calf for 18 to 24 months, the longest pregnancy period of any mammal. Then she gives birth while standing up.

Newborn calves are 3 feet (0.9 m) tall on average and weigh between 170 and 250 pounds (77–113.4 kg), depending on whether they are male or female. A newborn is mentally bright and alert, as its brain is already one-third the size of an adult elephant's brain. It knows nothing of the world, though, and must be taught everything about life in the herd. For the first four to five years of its life,

Elephants begin life having black hairs that are scattered across their dark gray skin, but the hairs wear off with age.

*Play is important to the social development of young elephants, who must learn their place in the herd's hierarchy.*

a young elephant is totally dependent on its mother for emotional and physical security.

Just as a human infant is fascinated with its own fingers and toes, so is a baby elephant curious about what to do with its amazing trunk. The calf relies on its mother to teach it how to use its trunk to pick up things, to scratch its ear, or to suck up water for a drink. In addition, by mimicking adults, calves learn how to give themselves dust baths, how to select the best food, and how to make the various elephant sounds that signal safety, excitement, and danger. All members of the herd work together to care for young elephants and keep them safe from predators such as lions and hyenas.

Because elephants are mammals, they nurse their young with milk. A short baby elephant may need to stand up on its hind legs to reach its mother's milk, which comes from two glands just behind the mother's front legs. Baby elephants live on milk for the first several months. Then they begin eating grass and leaves provided by their mothers. Eventually, milk becomes only a minor part of a calf's diet, but it may take up to 10 years (or until the birth of a sister or brother) for a calf to stop nursing from its mother.

Once an elephant has learned all it needs to know and can find its own food, it is ready to become a working member of the herd. Females stay close to their mothers throughout life and interact more than males within the family herd. They will also help raise new calves. Young males usually move away from their mothers earlier in life to join bull bands.

Elephants forage for food almost constantly—about 20 hours a day. During the hottest part of the day, they seek out water for drinking and bathing. Elephants splash and spray themselves and each other, coating their bodies with cool mud whenever it is available. During the day, dry dust baths help keep insects off the elephants' hides.

Napping is also part of an elephant's life. Elephants can remain standing while napping, but to sleep deeply, they must lie down. Elephants sleep only three or four hours a night, and only two of those hours are spent lying down. An elephant uses its trunk to gather up grass and leaves to make a pillow for its head. The entire herd never sleeps at the same time; a few elephants take turns standing guard against danger.

**African elephants make their own sunscreen by using their trunks to spray themselves first with water and then with a layer of dust.**

*When elephant herds travel, they sometimes walk in single file, with the babies hooked together, trunks to tails.*

Whether elephants are eating, bathing, or resting, they communicate with each other. They make quiet squeaks, low rumbles, and loud trumpets. In captivity, elephants have been known to mimic their keepers' voices and the sounds of machinery. Yet most of what elephants say is communicated using infrasound. The **frequencies** of these sound waves are so low that humans can't hear them. Scientists believe these sounds can travel as far as two and a half miles (4 km). This explains how males can find females for mating and how elephants that may have been separated from a migrating herd can find their way back to the herd.

Elephants travel hundreds of miles seasonally, depending on the availability of food and water.

While adult elephants have no natural predators (even lions seldom attack them), calves are vulnerable to attacks by crocodiles, hyenas, lions, and leopards. The greatest threat to all elephants in Africa and Asia is posed by humans. For hundreds of years, elephants have been hunted for their meat, hide, bones, and ivory tusks. Since 1989, hunting of the African elephant and ivory trading have been illegal, but professional traders have been trying to get such laws overturned.

*Wearing traditional costumes, mahouts in India still train and show elephants in ceremonies today.*

## WAR AND PEACE

The ancient Greek writer Homer was the first to write down stories about great "antlered beasts" from Asia—elephants—around 700 B.C. But elephants had been **domesticated** long before then. The history of elephant training in India and Southeast Asia goes back 4,000 years. Trainers, called *mahouts* in India, captured wild elephants and forced them to submit to commands. Skilled mahouts knew how to use nonviolent **conditioning** over several months to make elephants obey. Today, elephant training is considered an art in Asia, and the abilities of mahouts are highly valued.

Historically, Asian elephants were trained by native peoples to farm the land and assist with clearing trees. Visitors from other parts of the world were fascinated by the control that people had over these giant creatures. Then the foreigners quickly saw the potential elephants had for helping people overpower enemies. Rulers of the empires of China, Persia, and Rome hired mahouts and bought elephants to serve in their militaries.

Unlike horses, which were used for transportation, elephants served as weapons of war. They often wore

**The pad on the bottom of an elephant's foot elevates the back of the foot, causing elephants to walk on their tiptoes.**

*Images of elephants were carved on buildings' walls in Indian cities to show the people's respect for the animal.*

armored headpieces and breastplates. Spears were fastenened to their tusks, and loud bells were hung from their necks. Soldiers rode in large baskets on elephants' backs. Often, hundreds of elephants were lined up to form a barrier against **cavalry** attacks. Charging elephants stabbed men with their tusks and trampled them underfoot.

The most famous account of how elephants were used in battle is the story of Hannibal, a warlord from what is now the North African country of Tunisia. Hannibal led 50,000 soldiers and 37 elephants on a 15-day trek over the Alps mountain range into Italy to battle the Romans in 219 B.C. He lost thousands of men and 36 of the elephants to bad weather and hostile mountain tribes, but Hannibal's army defeated the Romans in two battles and was successful in taking northern Italy from Roman rule. When gunpowder came into wide use in the 1400s, elephants ceased to be helpful in battle. Instead, armies used them for transportation, and royalty displayed them as symbols of their power.

Elephants were also given as gifts among kings and other leaders. In A.D. 798, an elephant was given to soon-to-be Holy Roman emperor Charlemagne by the ruler

Called the "father of military strategy," Hannibal was known for many war tactics, including his use of elephants.

# THE DESOLATE VALLEY

Then, couched at night in hunter's wattled shieling,
How wildly beautiful it was to hear
The elephant his shrill reveille pealing
Like some far signal trumpet on the ear!
While the broad midnight moon was shining clear,
How fearful to look forth upon the woods,
And see those stately forest-kings appear,
Emerging from their shadowy solitudes—
As if that trump had woke Earth's old gigantic broods.

Such the majestic, melancholy scene
Which 'midst that mountain wilderness we found;
With scarce a trace to tell where man had been,
Save the old Kafir cabins crumbling round.
Yet this lone glen (Sicana's ancient ground)
To Nature's savage tribes abandoned long,
Had heard, erewhile, the Gospel's joyful sound,
And low of herds mixed with the Sabbath song.
But all is silent now. The Oppressor's hand was strong.

*Thomas Pringle (1789–1834)*
*excerpt from "The Desolate Valley"*

of Baghdad (a city in present-day Iraq). The rare white elephant was named Abul-Abbas. In 1255, Louis IX of France gave an elephant to Henry III of England as an addition to his royal **menagerie**. And in the 16th century, Pope Leo X kept a pet elephant named Hanno.

In the 17th century, performing elephants appeared in traveling zoos around Europe. Two hundred years later, elephants became popular circus performers and zoo attractions in North America. Probably the most famous circus elephant was Jumbo, the largest elephant in the world at that time. Entertainer P. T. Barnum paid $10,000 for Jumbo in 1882 and spent $20,000 to ship the elephant from Europe to America for his Barnum & Bailey Circus. Barnum's circus was advertised as the "Greatest Show on Earth," and Jumbo was its star, taking center ring of the new three-ring circus.

Jumbo traveled with Barnum & Bailey's for only three years. In 1885, tragedy struck when the circus was loading its train cars in the Canadian town of St. Thomas. As legend has it, an unscheduled train hurtled down the tracks toward the waiting animals, and a dwarf elephant named Tom Thumb stood in harm's way. Jumbo wrapped

**Small blood vessels in elephants' ears distribute heat so that it does not concentrate in one spot and cause the animal to overheat.**

*In New Delhi, the capital city of India, costumed elephants symbolize national pride and power in parades.*

his trunk around Tom Thumb and tossed him to safety, but Jumbo could not move out of the train's path in time. He was crushed and died on the tracks. A statue of Jumbo was later erected at the rail yard in St. Thomas.

Fictional elephants have been equally celebrated over the years. British author Rudyard Kipling was born in Mumbai (also called Bombay), India, and grew up around elephants and other wild animals. He wrote many stories featuring elephant characters, including "The Elephant's Child," a tale explaining why the elephant's trunk is so long. His most famous work, *The Jungle Book* (1894), included an elephant character named Hathi. In the 1930s, French writer Jean de Brunhoff created a series of stories about Babar, a young elephant who was named after a great Indian emperor. The following decade, Horton the elephant first appeared in the works of American author Dr. Seuss. In 2008, the animated film *Horton Hears a Who* retold the story of how the compassionate elephant struggles to save the tiny world of Who-ville.

According to ancient **Hindu** tradition, elephants were used to carry Indra, the King of the Gods. For this reason, the Asian elephant often figures into Hindu celebrations that involve costumes and music. For example, in cities throughout India and Southeast Asia, great elephant marches are held as part of various festivals and Hindu holidays. Elephants are decorated with elaborate velvet and silk fabrics, and their trunks, foreheads, and feet are brightly painted. They are draped from tusk to tail with jewels that jangle musically as

*The Hindu elephant god Ganesha is honored as one who helps people experience success in new undertakings.*

A pair of tusks from a male African elephant may be as heavy as 440 pounds (200 kg) and nearly 8 feet (2.4 m) long.

they walk. Contests are held, races are run, and games are played with the elephants.

Not all people respect elephants, though. The practice of ivory hunting began when Europeans moved into Africa and Asia in the 1800s. By 1850, England had **colonized** most of India, and European settlers began moving into East Africa around 1900. Adventurous hunters noticed the massive herds of large animals that were spread across the land. These men, called "white hunters," led hunting tours, or safaris, into the then-untamed lands of Kenya, Nairobi, Tanzania, and Uganda. Millionaires, royalty, and movie stars accompanied the white hunters in search of big game such as elephants.

It was not uncommon in those days for hunters to obtain African elephant tusks that weighed nearly 300 pounds (136 kg). In Asia and Africa, millions of elephants—and other animals—were carelessly slaughtered between 1850 and 1980, when concerns about species destruction finally emerged. Despite a worldwide ban on ivory that has been in place since 1989, **poachers** continue to hunt elephants. Today, fewer than 400,000 elephants roam the African landscape.

By the 1900s, southern Africa's elephants were nearly wiped out due to foreign hunting expeditions.

Elephants that live in protected but open areas can be more easily studied and tracked by scientists.

## ON THE BRINK

While research and breeding programs keep captive elephants all over the world, scientists and conservationists know that protecting elephants in their own habitats is vital to elephants' survival. In 2002, the United States signed into law a new version of the African Elephant Conservation Act. It provides annual funding to countries in which elephants live. Using these funds, governments establish protected areas, pay rangers to patrol the land for poachers, and establish research groups to monitor elephant populations.

The World Wildlife Fund, supported by more than 100 nations, can conduct research on a larger scale. One of its projects is the **satellite** tracking of forest elephants in West Africa. To monitor individual elephants, scientists first shoot them with tranquilizer darts to make them fall asleep. After about 20 minutes, when a darted elephant finally falls asleep, researchers pour water over its ears to keep it cool while they go to work on it. Skin and blood samples are taken, and a special collar is placed around its neck. The collar has a **Global Positioning System** (GPS) tracking device on it. When researchers

The stuffed body of the largest African elephant ever recorded can be seen at the National Museum of Natural History in Washington, D.C.

*Elephants can reach food that is 20 feet (6 m) off the ground, making them among the world's most versatile herbivores.*

are finished, they inject the elephant with a substance to make it wake up.

The information gathered from the GPS devices helps researchers count herd populations and understand how and where the elephants migrate during the seasons. It also helps predict which elephants will likely come into conflict with humans and in what areas elephants are most vulnerable to poachers. Additional protected areas can then be established to give elephants the space they need to roam.

Elephants need to have access to large areas of land to survive; therefore, in addition to hunting, habitat loss is a major factor in the decline of elephant populations. Human **encroachment** in both Asia and Africa has put people in closer contact with elephants as the animals search smaller habitats for food and water. The spread of urban areas has blocked migration routes, causing delays and confusion for elephants.

Building farms closer to elephant habitats leads to problems such as crop raiding. Research to discover methods to keep elephants from raiding crops is conducted by environmental and agricultural groups in both Africa and Asia. When elephants trample or

eat crops, angered farmers may either kill the elephants illegally or trap them and sell them to "elephant camps." These are places where elephants are put on display and sometimes trained to do tricks for the amusement of tourists. Unfortunately, elephants are often overcrowded and may be abused in such camps.

Abuse and **trauma**, scientists now believe, leads to changes in normal elephant behavior. In studies conducted by the National Geographic Society and by universities in Oregon and California, scientists found

*To save elephants from human threats, wildlife managers often capture and relocate elephants to protected areas.*

*Confining elephants to safe environments is not always easy, as they sometimes try to escape captivity.*

that young elephants who witness the slaughter of their herds by ivory poachers and are left as orphans grow up confused and angry. These elephants can carry the memories of traumatic events with them throughout their lives, suffering from depression and exhibiting violent behavior similar to the symptoms of post-traumatic stress disorder (PTSD) that humans suffer after witnessing serious destruction, war, or death. Yet leading elephant experts such as psychologist Dr. Gay Bradshaw believe that elephants can recover from PTSD if humans give them the proper care and support. Bradshaw and others who have dedicated their lives to studying elephant behavior think that elephants have the capacity to forgive and move past traumatic experiences.

Further studies of the inner workings of elephants' minds have been conducted by scientist Joyce Poole. She studied elephants at Amboseli National Park, at the foot of Mt. Kilimanjaro in Kenya, for more than 30 years. Poole and others' work with the Amboseli Elephant Research Project—which was established in 1972 and is the longest-running study of elephants in the world—has led to invaluable discoveries about the relationships and social behavior of elephants, as well as their reproductive patterns and communication. Specifically, Poole's research has revealed that elephants can recognize themselves in a mirror, which means they are self-aware—a trait that, until recently, scientists thought only humans, apes, and dolphins possessed. In addition, elephants can use tools, a behavior that is rare in the animal kingdom. Elephants have been observed piling up tires to use as steps to reach high branches, and they have used logs to short out electric fences.

Research projects sponsored by the National Science Foundation and conducted at zoos around the world, as well as at Amboseli, revealed that in addition to communicating with infrasound, elephants also use chemical signals. Their bodily fluids—tears, sweat, and urine—have smells that are unique to each elephant. Scientists believe that since elephants can recognize the smell of family members, the chemical signals prevent males from choosing a close relative when they mate with females. Research on elephant communication helps scientists understand social bonding and the importance of preserving family groups.

The African elephant's ears can grow to be six feet (2 m) long, while the Asian elephant's are only two feet (61 cm) long.

*Elephants can use their trunks to do many things, even painting.*

**Ruby, an Asian elephant who lived at the Phoenix Zoo in Phoenix, Arizona, for 24 years, became famous for her paintings.**

For those elephants that cannot be protected in the wild, there are special sanctuaries where they can be taken for safekeeping. The Elephant Sanctuary in Hohenwald, Tennessee, is a refuge developed especially for **displaced** elephants. The sanctuary rescues old, sick, or emotionally damaged elephants that would otherwise be killed. In Hohenwald, elephants are not put on display but are allowed to live in peace on 2,700 acres (1,093 ha) of forest and plains.

Many zoos and animal parks also promote conservation. African Lion Safari, a "drive-through" wildlife park in Ontario, Canada, educates the public through the experiences visitors have with its animals. While visitors remain "caged" inside their vehicles, the animals roam freely. The International Elephant Foundation is one of many organizations whose goal is to support elephant conservation through worldwide education.

Even though elephant populations are a fraction of what they were less than half a century ago, some places have more elephants than populated areas can support. The African Wildlife Foundation and numerous organizations in Asia work to relocate elephants to

natural habitats and to find ways for humans to peacefully coexist with elephants. With further education, stronger international laws, and financial support, such organizations can continue to help elephants survive in a rapidly changing world.

Scientists believe that mammoths spent much of their time in the water and passed that trait down to elephants.

## ANIMAL TALE: THE WHITE ELEPHANT

**Elephants are considered sacred, or holy, creatures in India. Symbols of strength and honor, elephants have been part of Indian folklore for 5,000 years. The story of the white elephant illustrates this animal's important status as an intelligent, kind, and noble creature.**

A long time ago in India, there lived a magnificent white elephant who loved his mother. She had grown old and gone blind, so the young elephant promised to care for her all the days of her life. The elephant took his mother to Mount Candorana to live in a cave beside a calm lake covered with pink flowers called lotuses. His mother was happy there, and this made the white elephant happy.

One day, the white elephant heard someone crying in the forest. He found a man who explained that he had come from Benaras, India's sacred capital city, to visit relatives. But now, after seven days of wandering alone, he was frightened, tired, and hungry, and he could not find his way out of the forest. "I will help you," the elephant told the man. He then lifted the man onto his back and took him to the edge of the forest.

When the man got home to Benaras, he learned that the royal elephant belonging to King Brahmadutta had just died. The king sent out a decree to everyone in the kingdom: "We must find a new royal elephant. He must be brave, and strong, and beautiful to serve the king." So the man rushed to tell the king of the white elephant living on Mount Candorana. This news pleased the king greatly, and he sent the man and several mahouts on a mission to capture this elephant.

In the forest, the group sneaked up behind the white elephant and trapped him. The elephant felt betrayed by the man he had helped, but he did not resist. He knew that if he struggled, the men might be hurt—and he was too kindhearted to hurt anyone.

That night, when the white elephant did not return home, his mother wept bitterly.

In the city of Benaras, the king was thrilled. He ordered his people to shower the elephant with flowers and paint his skin bright colors. The best food was served, but the elephant refused to even taste it.

The king asked the elephant why he was not happy to be the royal elephant. The elephant explained that he wanted only to care for his blind mother back on Mount Candorana; he could not eat or celebrate knowing that his mother was alone and starving.

The king, touched by the elephant's story, set the elephant free. The happy elephant rushed home and found his mother asleep in the cave. When he stroked her face, she awoke and cried out with joy. He told her how he had been captured by the king's men and how the king had set him free. His mother was overjoyed to have her son back and blessed the king with peace, prosperity, and joy for the rest of his life.

The white elephant cared for his mother until the day she died. And when he died many years later, the king erected a statue of him. To this day, the city (now called Varanasi) holds an annual elephant festival to honor the white elephant's kind and noble soul.

## GLOSSARY

**adaptation** – a change in a species to improve its chances of survival in its environment

**cavalry** – soldiers that fight on horseback

**colonized** – established settlements in a new land and exercised control over them

**conditioning** – a process of training living things to behave in a certain way

**displaced** – forced to leave one's home due to destruction or disaster

**DNA** – deoxyribonucleic acid; a substance found in every living thing that determines the species and individual characteristics of that thing

**domesticated** – tamed to be kept as a pet or used as a work animal

**encroachment** – movement into the space of another

**extinction** – the act or process of becoming extinct; coming to an end or dying out

**frequencies** – the measurements of sound waves

**Global Positioning System** – a system of satellites, computers, and other electronic devices that work together to determine the location of objects or living things that carry a trackable device

**hierarchy** – a system in which people, animals, or things are ranked in importance one above another

**Hindu** – relating to Hinduism, the third-largest religion in the world

**mammoths** – elephant-like mammals of the extinct class *Mammuthus*; mammoths had fur and ridged teeth

**menagerie** – a collection of wild or unique animals that are kept on display

**poachers** – people who hunt protected species of wild game and fish, even though doing so is against the law

**satellite** – a mechanical device launched into space; it may be designed to travel around Earth or toward other planets or the sun

**trauma** – a physical or emotional wound or shock so painful that it causes lasting damage to the victim

## SELECTED BIBLIOGRAPHY

African Wildlife Foundation. "Conserving Wildlife: Elephants." AWF. http://www.awf.org/section/wildlife/elephants.

Bloom, Steve. *Elephant*. San Francisco: Chronicle Books, 2005.

ElephantVoices. "Homepage." Elephant Voices. http://www.elephantvoices.org.

Moss, Cynthia. *Elephant Memories: Thirteen Years in the Life of an Elephant Family*. Chicago: University of Chicago Press, 2000.

O'Connell, Caitlin. *The Elephant's Secret Sense: The Hidden Life of the Wild Herds of Africa*. New York: Free Press, 2007.

U.S. Fish and Wildlife Service, International Affairs. "Wildlife without Borders: African Elephant Program." http://www.fws.gov/international/afecf/afecf.htm.

*A calf learns everything it needs to know about life from its mother or another older female relative.*

# INDEX